AF326838

Bryan Hunt

Recent Drawings

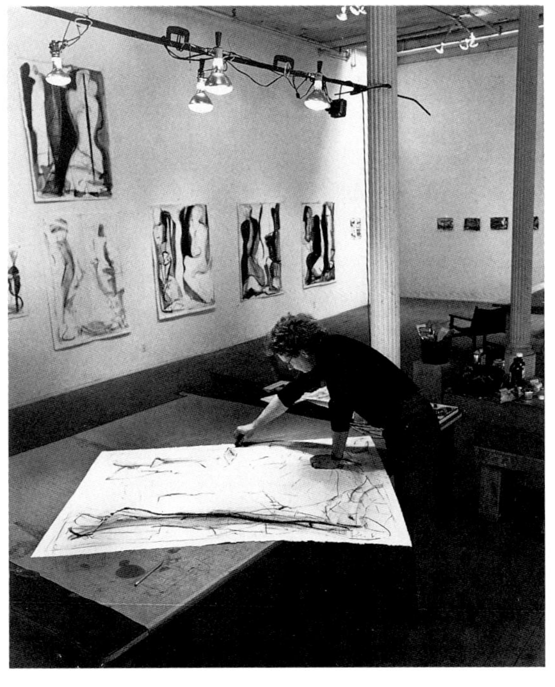

Bryan Hunt

Recent Drawings

5–29 April, 1989

BlumHelman 20 West 57th Street, New York, NY 10019

Luna y Mar, II, III, VI, 1989
oilstick and pencil on 100% cotton black paper
11 × 15″ each
(suite of 6 drawings)

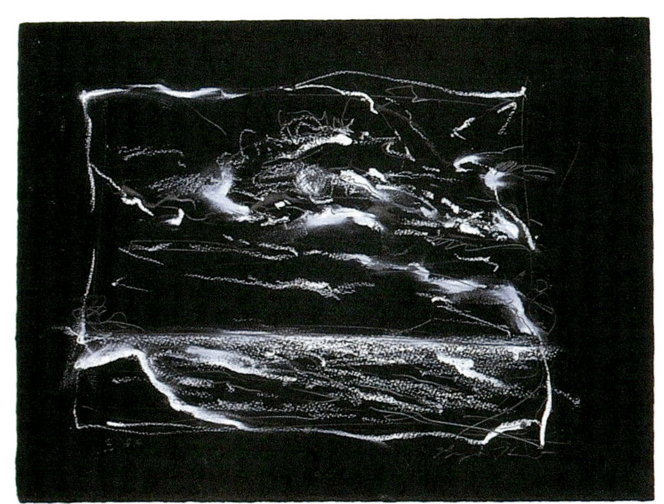

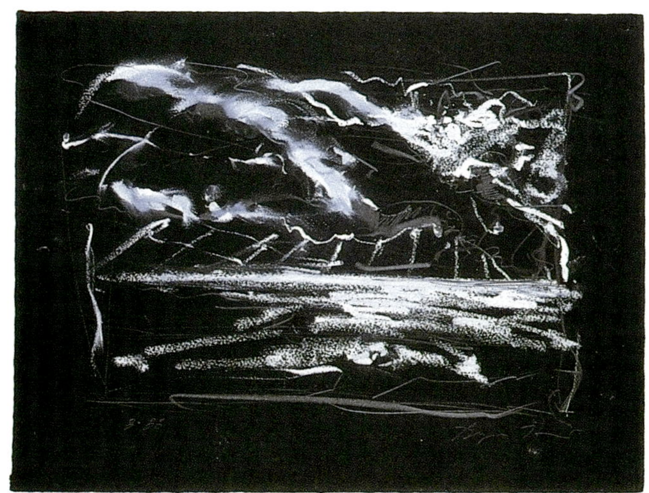

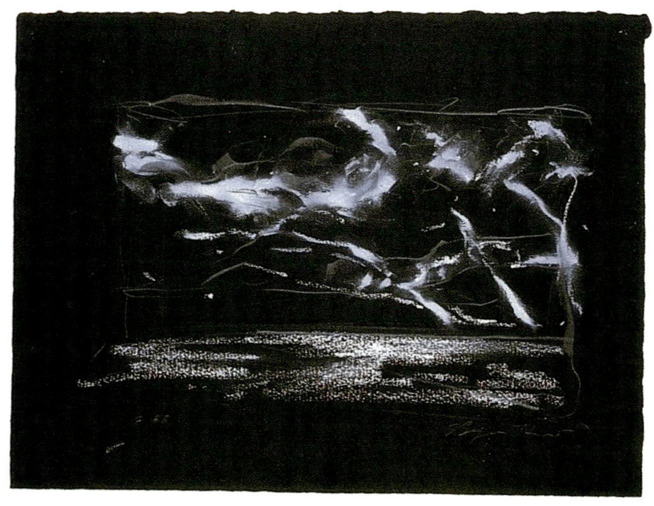

Canyon I, 1988
graphite, linseed oil, wax, pigment and
conte crayon on Arches paper
22 × 30″

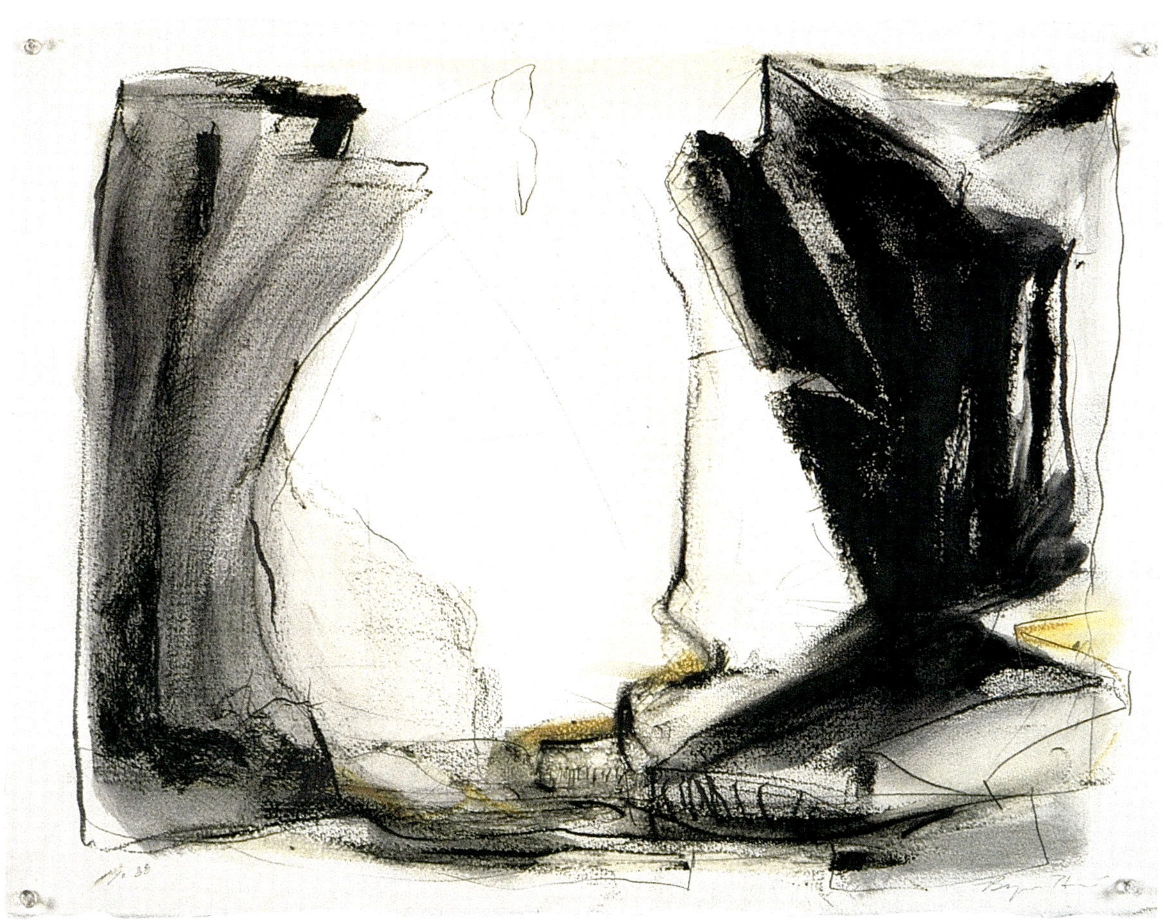

Siesta I, II, 1989
watercolor, graphite, oilstick and conte crayon
on Arches paper
15 × 11¼" each
(series of 5 drawings)

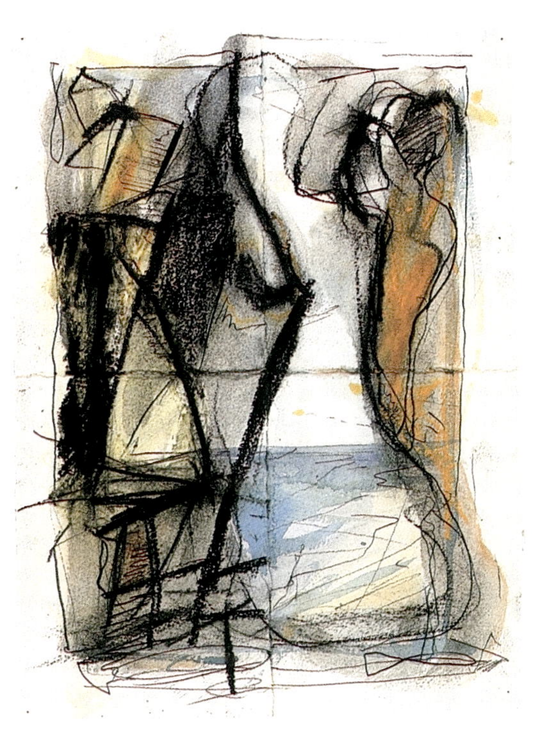 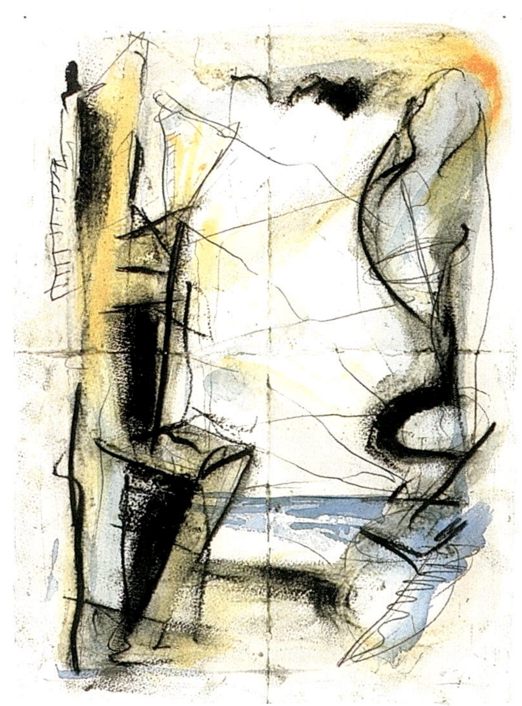

Siesta III, IV, 1989
watercolor, graphite, oilstick and conte crayon
on Arches paper
15 × 11¼″
(series of 5 drawings each)

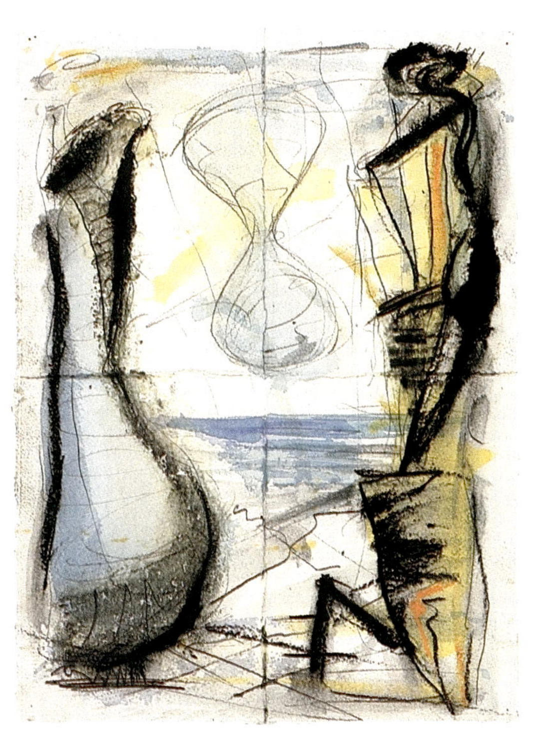 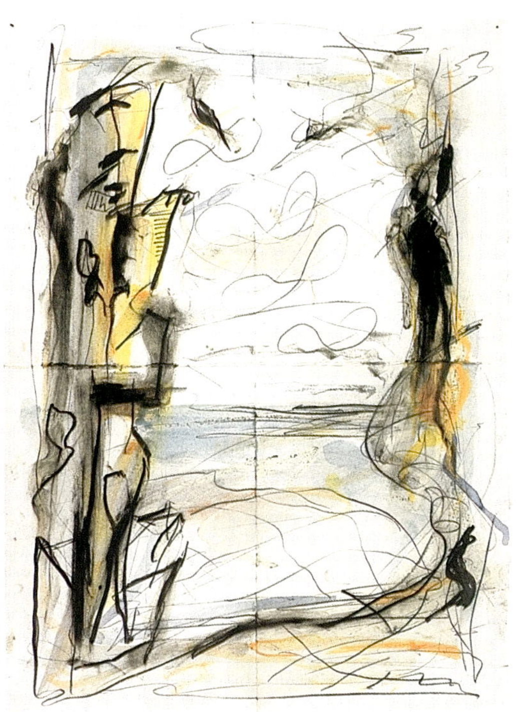

Quarryscape I, 1988
graphite and oilstick on Arches paper
22¾ × 15″

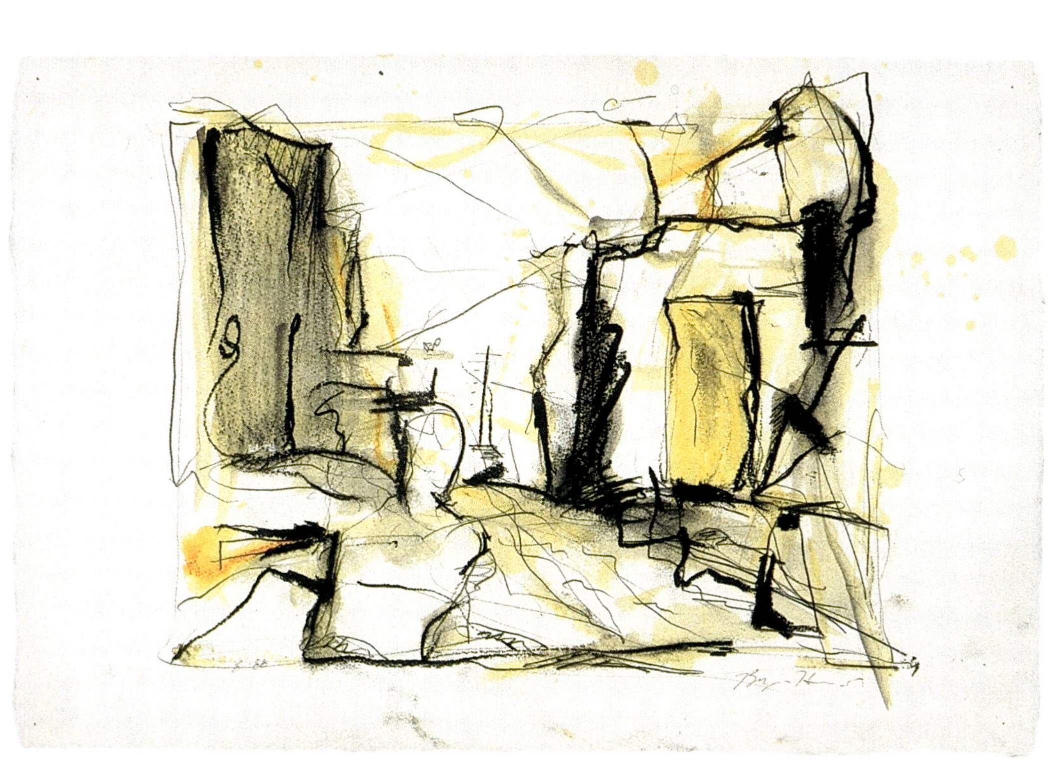

Punta del Cantal I, II, 1989
watercolor, graphite and oilstick
on Arches paper
11¼ × 15″ each
(series of 4 drawings)

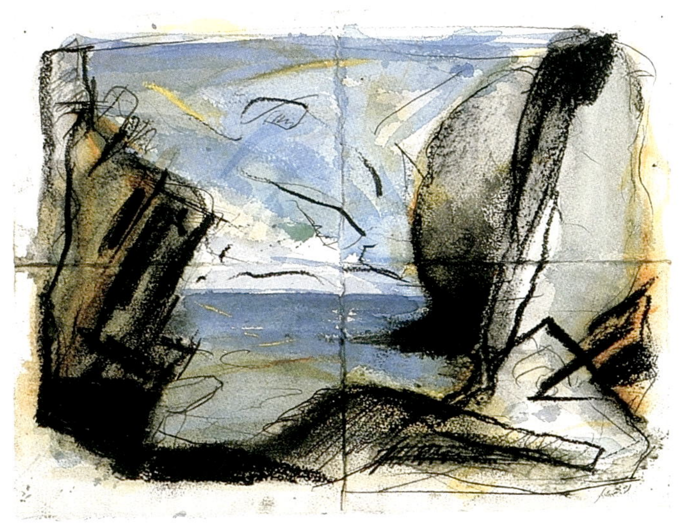

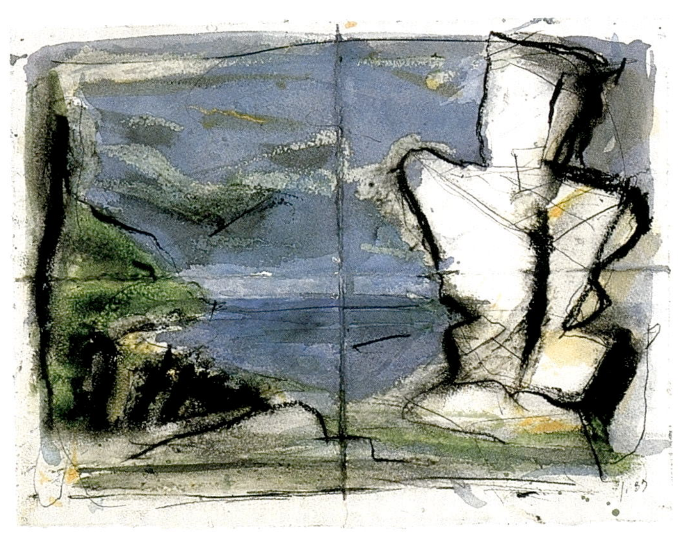

Punta del Cantal III, IV, 1989
watercolor, graphite and oilstick
on Arches paper
11¼ × 15″ each
(series of 4 drawings)

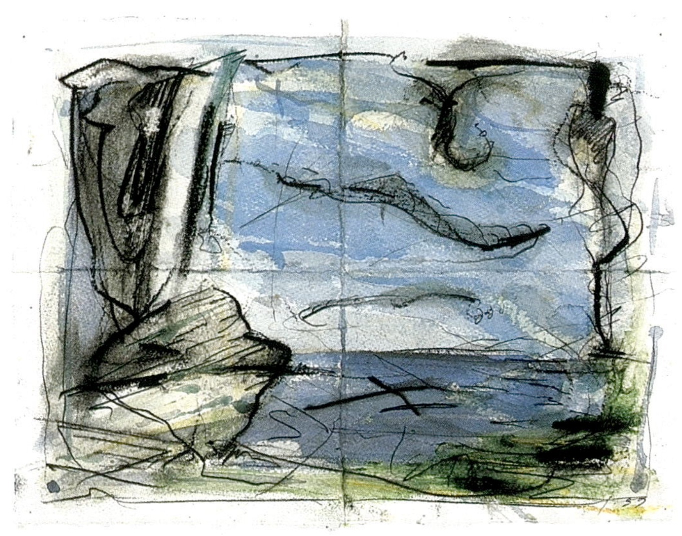

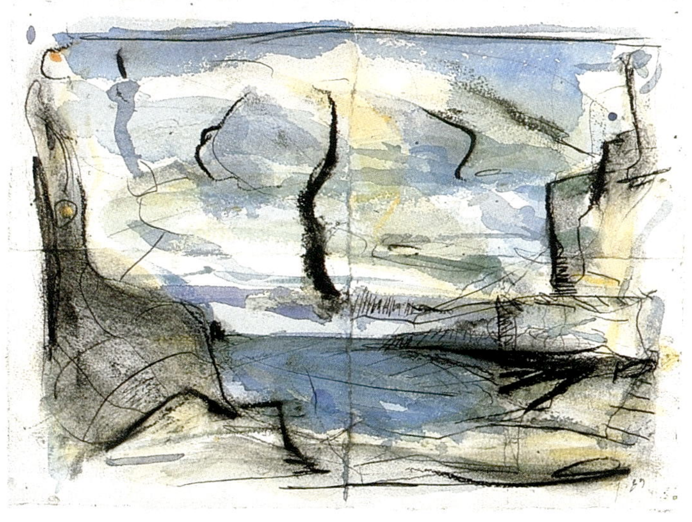

Myth I, 1989
graphite, linseed oil and conte crayon
on Arches paper
59½ × 45"

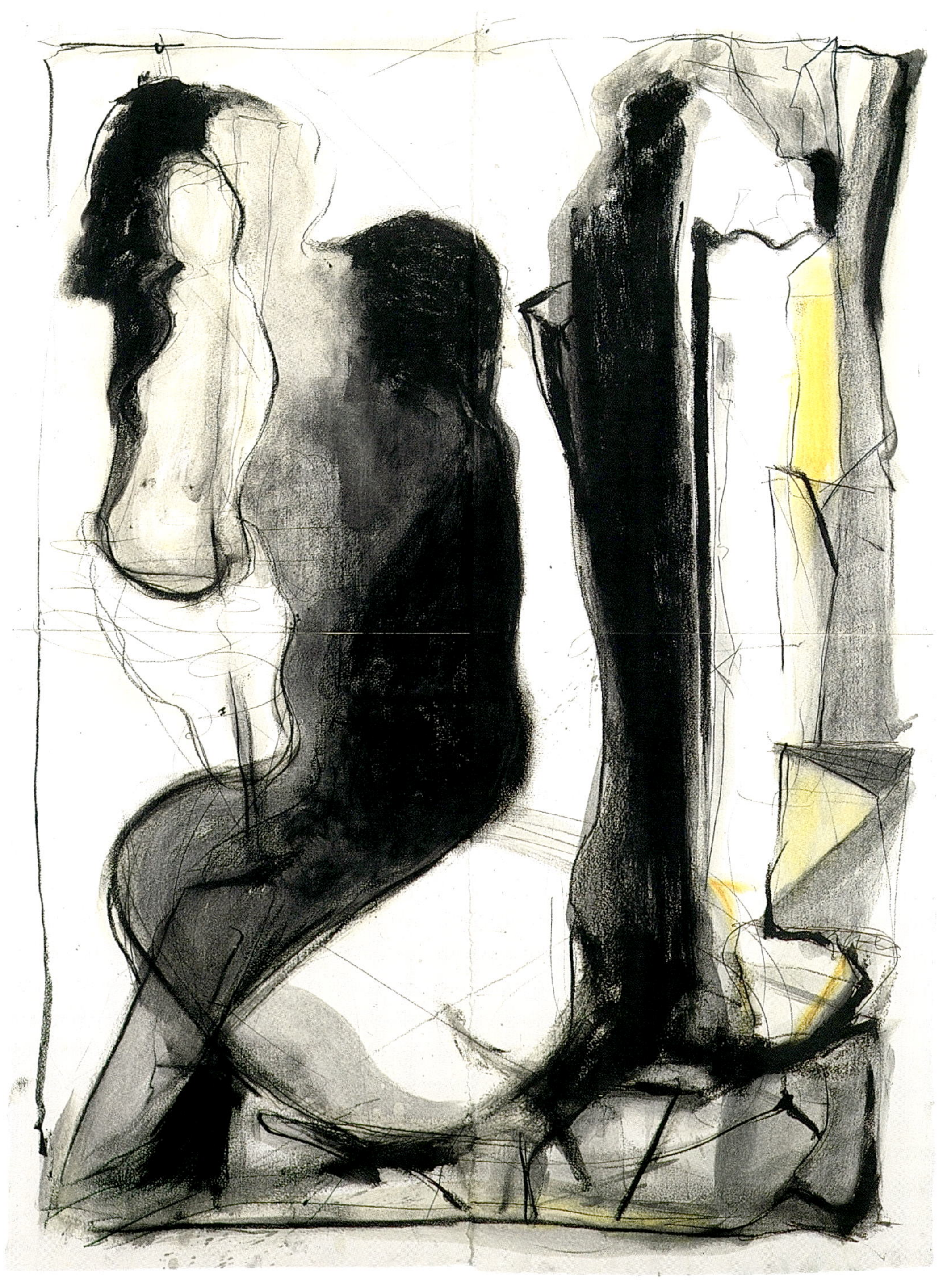

Coast Studies I–IV, 1989
watercolor, graphite, oilstick and conte crayon
on Arches paper
7½ × 7½" each
(suite of 4 drawings)

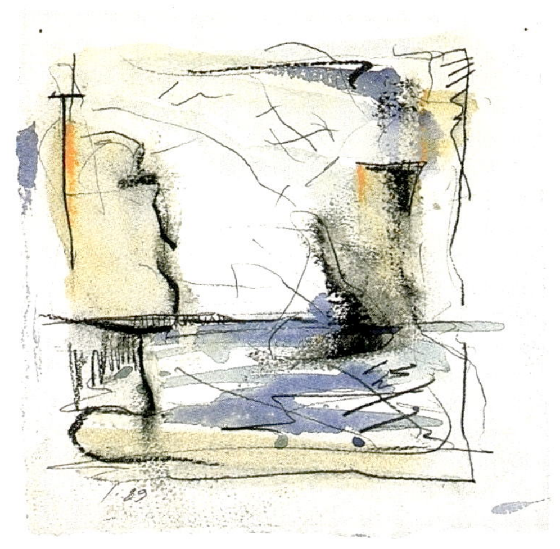

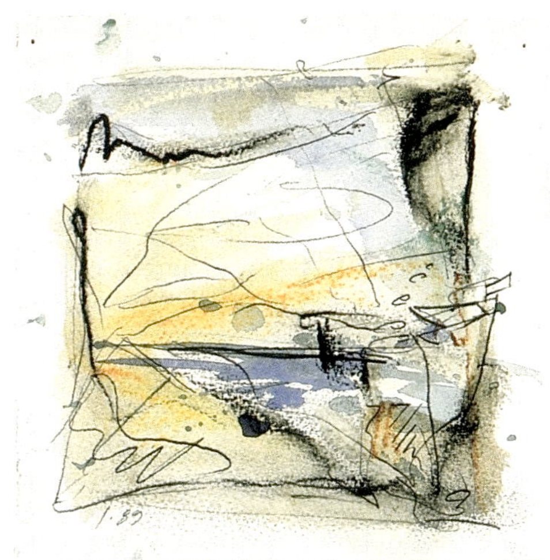

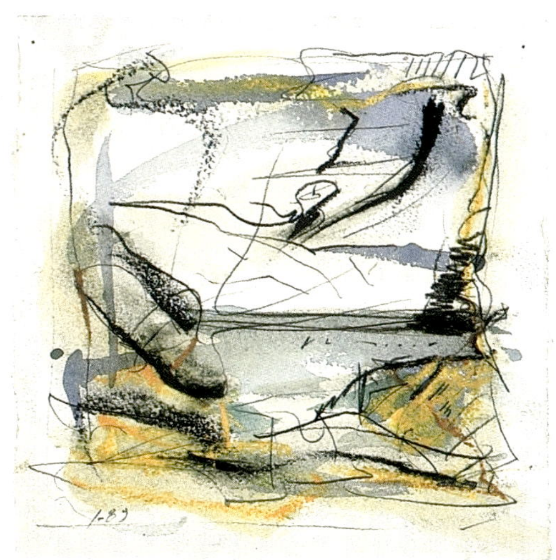

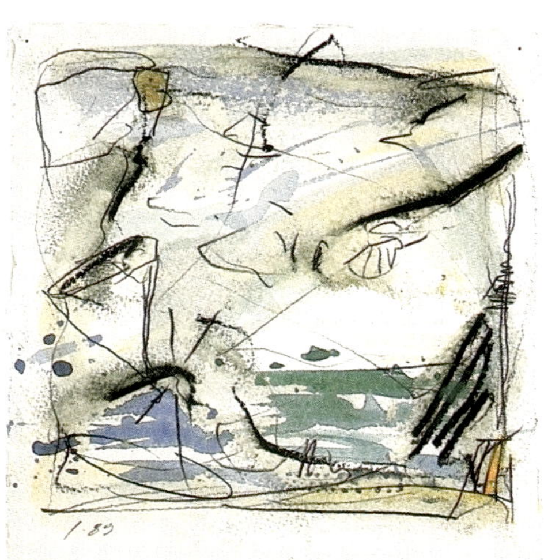

Canyon II, 1988
graphite, linseed oil, wax, pigment and
conte crayon on Arches paper
22 × 30″

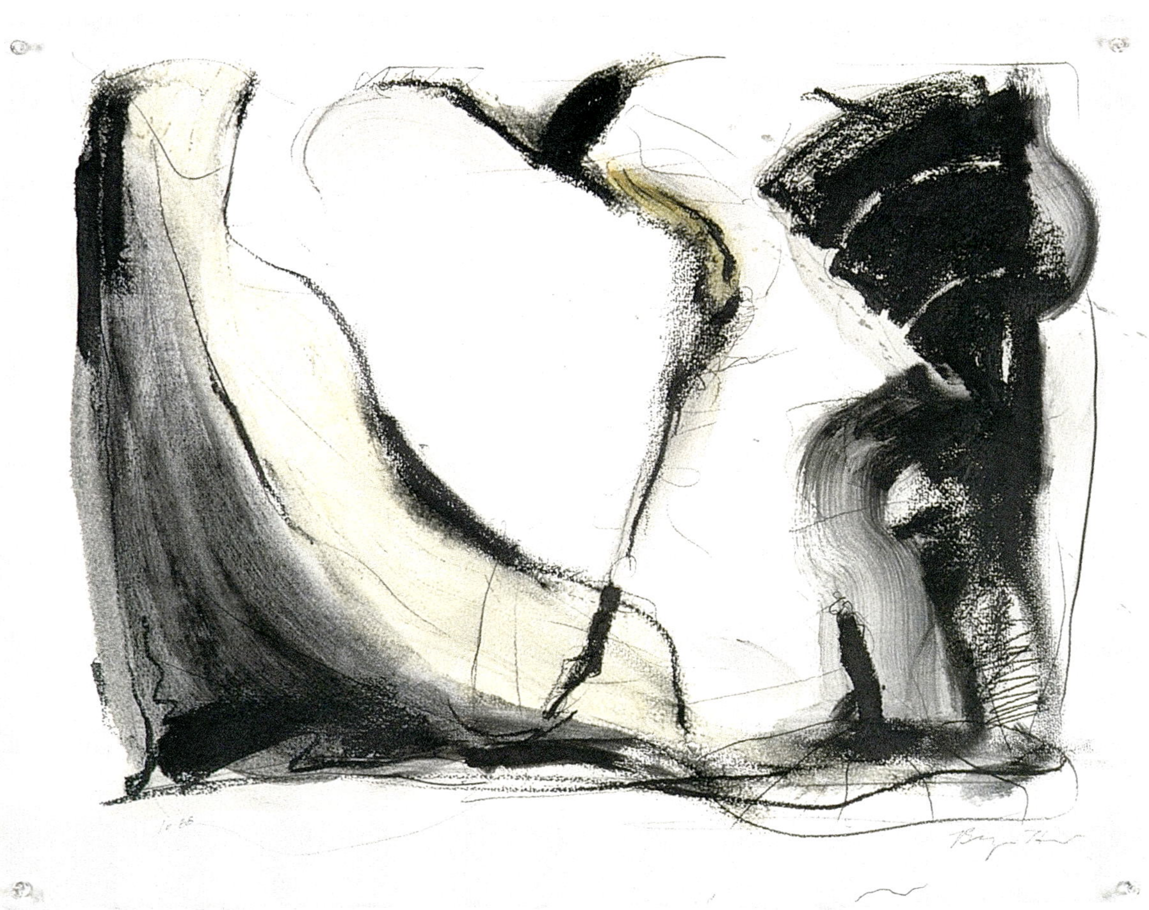

Myth III, 1989
graphite, linseed oil and watercolor on
Arches paper
59½ × 45"

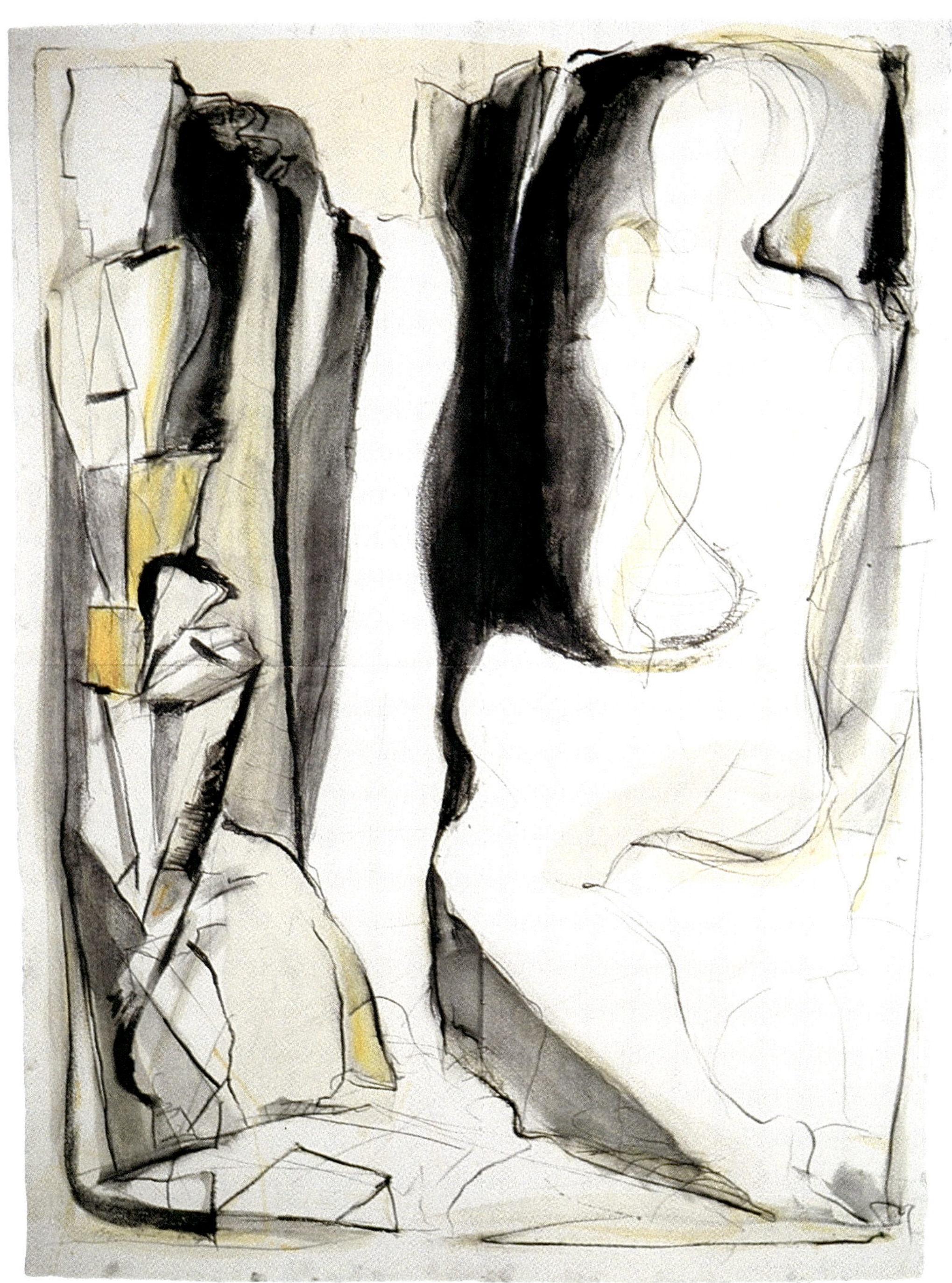

Quarry at Tuy I, II, 1988
graphite, watercolor and oilstick on Arches paper
11 × 15″ each
(series of 4 drawings)

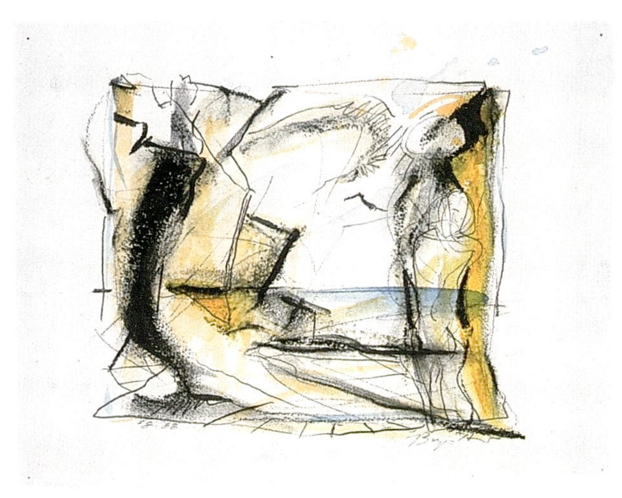

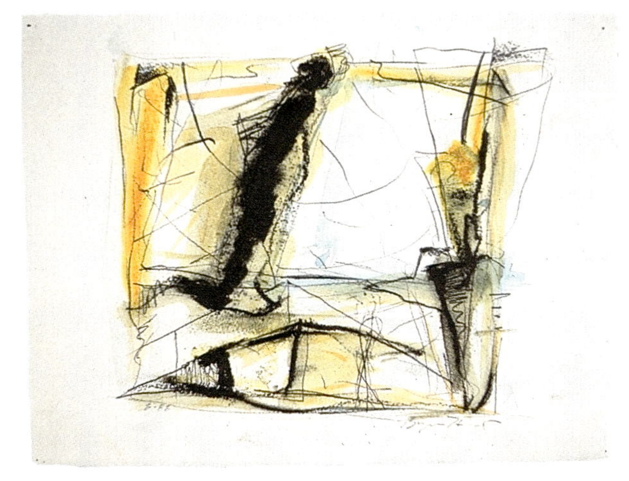

Quarry at Tuy III, IV, 1988
graphite, watercolor and oilstick on Arches paper
11 × 15″ each
(series of 4 drawings)

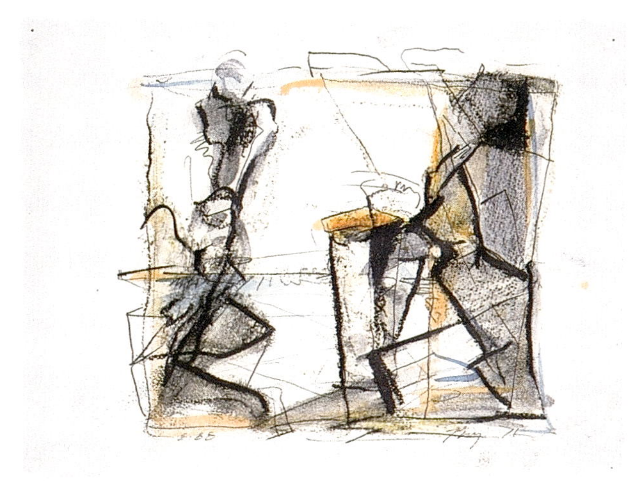

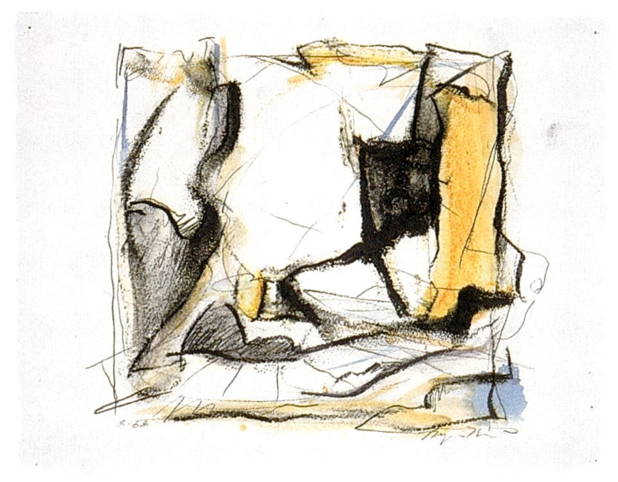

Barrier, 1988
graphite, linseed oil, pigment, wax and
charcoal on Arches paper
30 × 22"

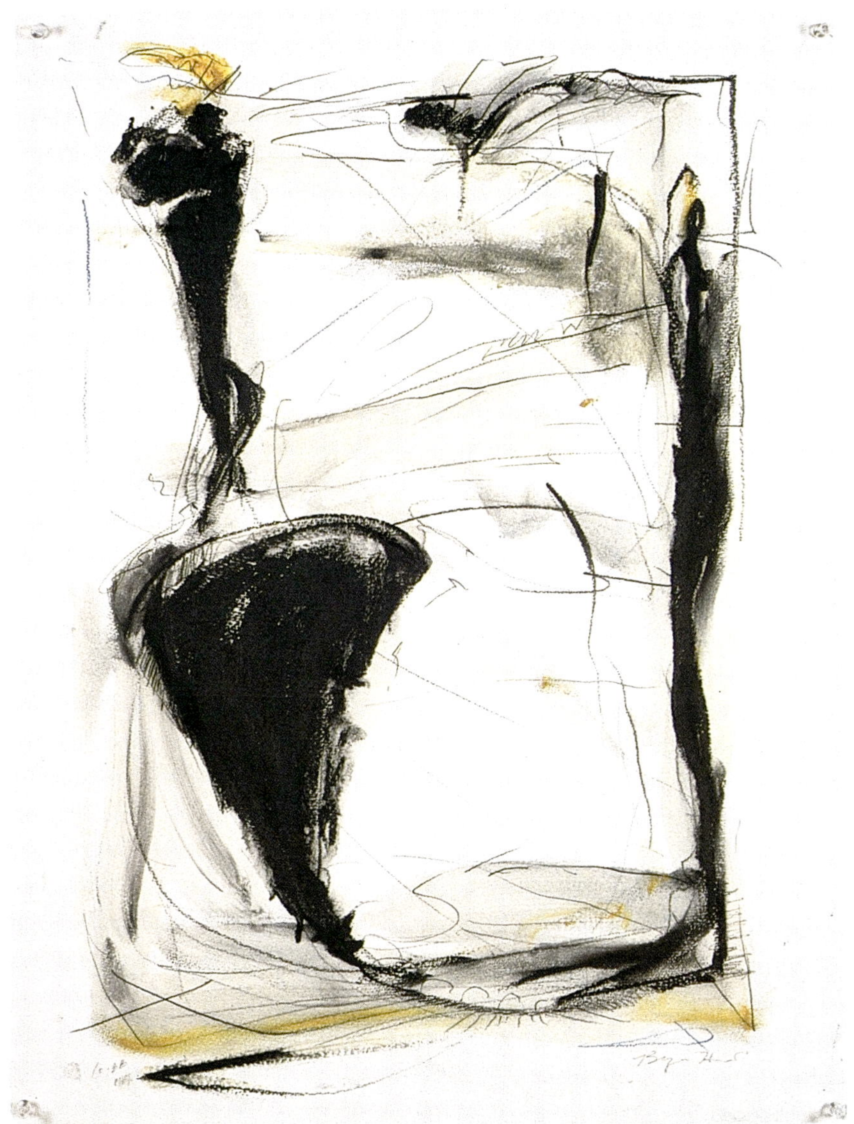

Red Studies I–IV, 1989
watercolor, graphite, oilstick and conte crayon
on Arches paper
7½ × 7½" each
(series of 4 drawings)

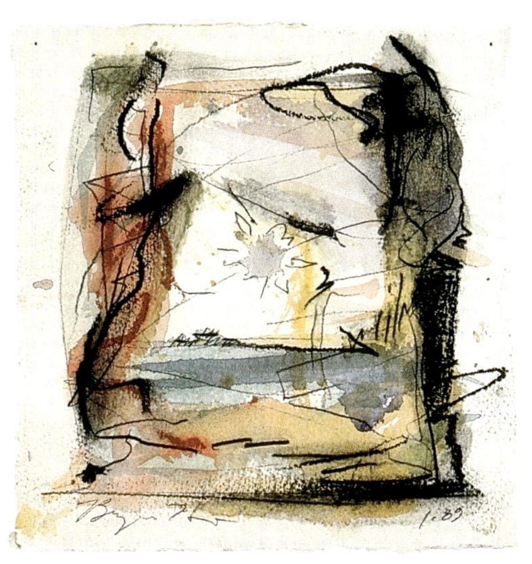

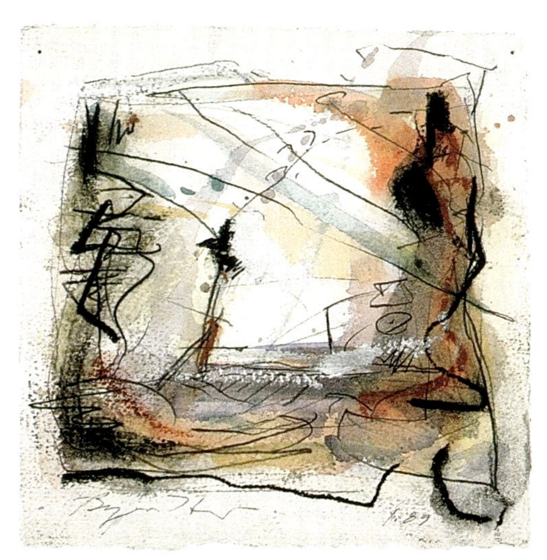

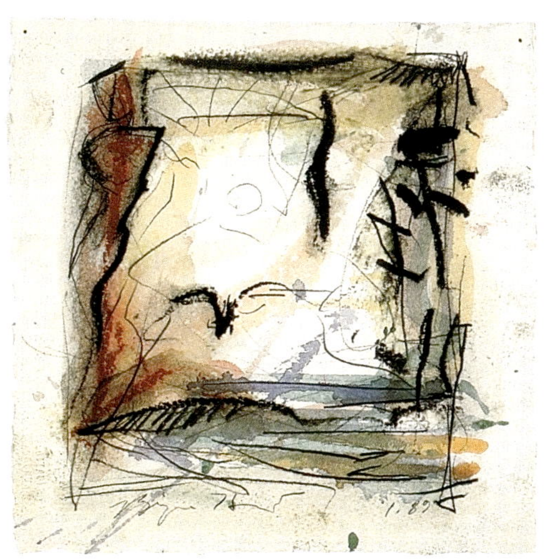

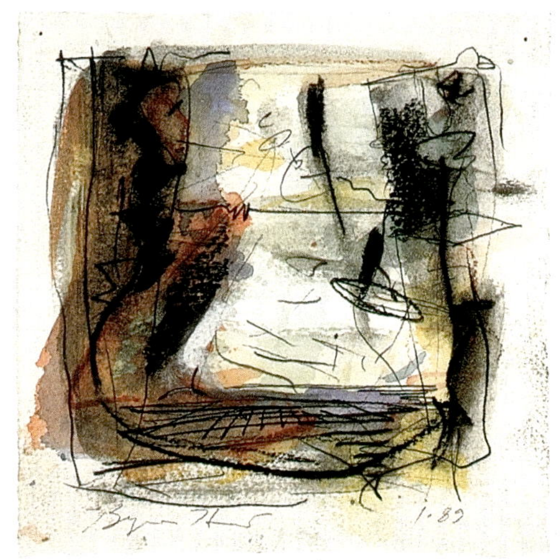

Nature Morte II, 1988
graphite, linseed oil, pigment, wax and
charcoal on Arches paper
30 × 22"

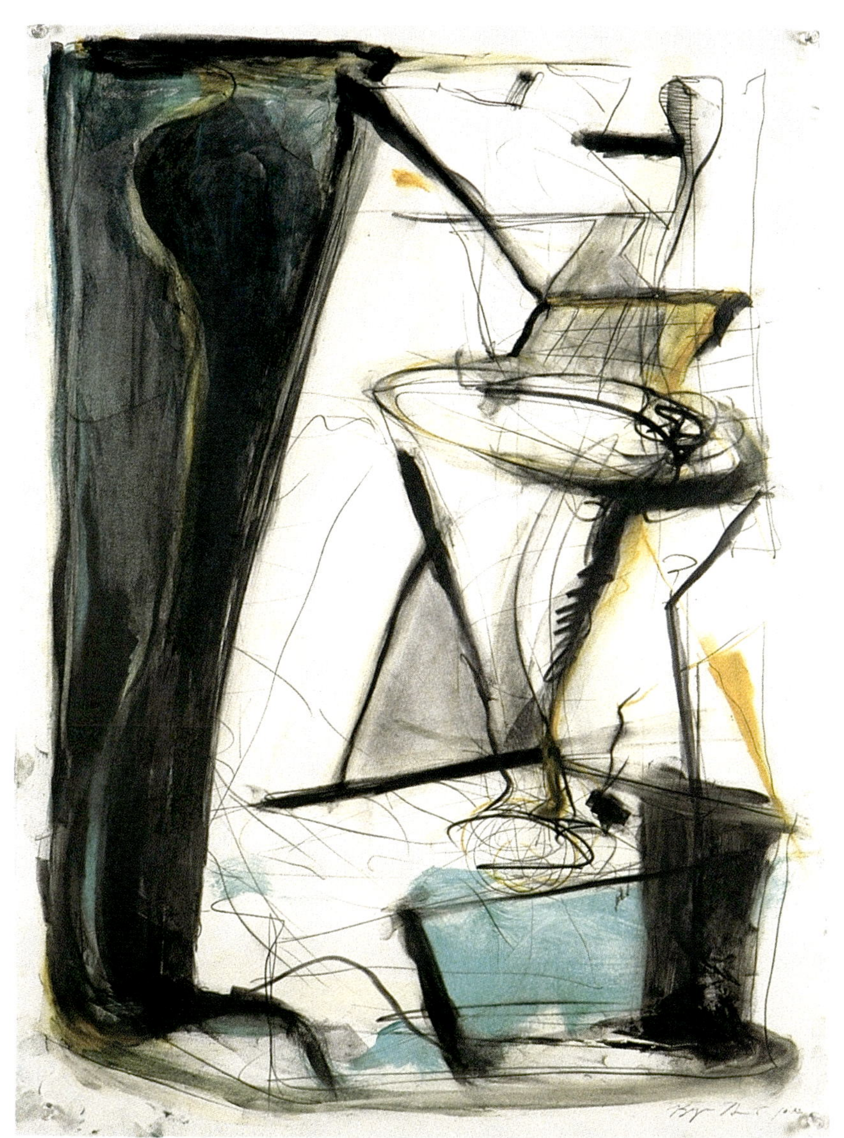

Bryan Hunt

1947

Born: Terre Haute, Indiana

Education

1969–71

B.F.A Otis Art Institute of Los Angeles

1972

Whitney Museum of American Art,
Independent Study Program

One-Person Exhibitions

1974

The Institute for Art and Urban Resources,
The Clocktower, New York
"C.B. Hunt: Recent Works"

Jack Glenn Gallery, Corona del Mar,
California
"Bryan Hunt"

1975

Palais des Beaux-Arts, Brussels
"C. Bryan Hunt: 'Empire State/Graf,'
'Phobos,' 'Universal Joint'"

1976

Daniel Weinberg Gallery, San Francisco
"Bryan Hunt: Sculpture"

1977

BlumHelman Gallery, New York
"Bryan Hunt: Sculpture"

1978

BlumHelman Gallery, New York
"Bryan Hunt: New Sculpture and
Drawings"

Daniel Weinberg Gallery, San Francisco
"Bryan Hunt: Sculpture and Drawings"

Greenberg Gallery, St. Louis
"Bryan Hunt: Sculpture"

1979

BlumHelman Gallery, New York
"Bryan Hunt: Recent Sculpture"

Bernard Jacobson, Ltd., London
"Bryan Hunt: Lakes·Waterfalls·Airships"

BlumHelman Gallery, New York
"Drawings"

Galerie Bischofberger, Zürich
"Bryan Hunt: Neue Werke"

1980

Margo Leavin Gallery, Los Angeles
"Bryan Hunt"

1981

Akron Art Institute, Ohio
"Bryan Hunt: Sculpture & Drawings"

BlumHelman Gallery, New York
"Bryan Hunt"

Galerie Hans Strelow, Düsseldorf
"Skulpturen und Zeichnungen"

1982

Daniel Weinberg Gallery, San Francisco
"Bryan Hunt: Sculpture & Drawings"

Bernier Gallery, Athens, Greece
"Drawings"

1983

BlumHelman Gallery, New York
(20 West 57th Street and 112 Greene Street)
"Bryan Hunt"

Margo Leavin Gallery, Los Angeles
"Bryan Hunt: Recent Sculpture"

Los Angeles County Museum of Art
"Gallery Six: Bryan Hunt"

Amerika Haus, Berlin
"New Masters: Bryan Hunt"

The University Art Museum, California
State University, Long Beach
"Bryan Hunt: A Decade of Drawings"

1984

John C. Stoller & Co., Minneapolis
"Bryan Hunt"

1985

Knoedler, Zürich
"Bryan Hunt: Skulpturen and
Zeichnungen"

BlumHelman Gallery, New York
Bryan Hunt: Recent Sculpture,
Including the Barcelona Series"

1986

Gillespie, Laage, Salomon, Paris
"Bryan Hunt: Sculptures"

Akira Ikeda Gallery, Tokyo
"Bryan Hunt: Sculptures & Drawings"

University Art Museum, University of
California, Berkeley
"MATRIX; Bryan Hunt Airships"

BlumHelman Gallery, New York
"Bryan Hunt: Recent Small-Scale Works"

Daniel Weinberg Gallery, Los Angeles
"Bryan Hunt Airships: 1974–1986"

1987

Barbara Mathes Gallery, New York
"Bryan Hunt: Drawings"

BlumHelman Warehouse, New York
"Bryan Hunt: Recent Sculpture"

Wilhelm-Lehmbruck-Museum, Duisburg,
West Germany
"Bryan Hunt: Skulpturen und
Zeichnungen"

1988

BlumHelman Los Angeles
"Bryan Hunt: Recent Sculpture"

Cornell University, Herbert F. Johnson
Museum of Art, Ithaca, New York
"Bryan Hunt: Falls and Figures"
Exhibition travelled: Fort Worth Art
Museum; Center for the Arts at
Muhlenberg College, Allentown,
Pennsylvania

Evelyn Aimis Fine Art, Toronto
"Bryan Hunt Sculptures and Drawings"

University of Rhode Island, Kingston
"Bryan Hunt: Earth and Air"

1989

BlumHelman Gallery, New York
"Recent Drawings"

Crown Point Press, New York
"Bryan Hunt"

Crown Point Press, San Francisco
"Bryan Hunt"

Galeria Arteunido, Barcelona
"Bryan Hunt"

Thomas Segal Gallery, Boston
"Bryan Hunt: Sculpture and Drawings"

Public Collections

Akron Museum of Art, Ohio

Albright-Knox Art Gallery, Buffalo, New York

Arkansas Art Center, Little Rock, Arkansas

Art Institute of Chicago

Dallas Museum of Art

Des Moines Art Center, Iowa

Fogg Art Museum, Cambridge, Massachusetts

Frank Lloyd Wright Fallingwater Conservancy,
Kaufman House, Bear Run, Pennsylvania

Herbert F. Johnson Museum of Art, Cornell University,
Ithaca, New York

The High Museum, Atlanta

Los Angeles County Museum of Art

Louisiana Museum of Modern Art, Humlebaek, Denmark

Massachusetts Institute of Technology, Cambridge

The Metropolitan Museum of Art, New York

The Museum of Contemporary Art, Los Angeles

The Museum of Fine Arts, Houston

The Museum of Modern Art, New York

National Museum of American Art, Washington, D.C.

The Newark Museum, New Jersey

Newport Harbor Museum, Newport Beach, California

St. Louis Museum, Missouri

San Francisco Museum of Modern Art

The Solomon R. Guggenheim Museum, New York

Stedelijk Museum, Amsterdam, The Netherlands

Vassar College Art Gallery, Poughkeepsie, New York

Whitney Museum of American Art, New York

Wilhelm-Lehmbruck-Museum, Duisburg, West Germany

Yale University Art Gallery, New Haven, Connecticut

Published on the occasion of
Bryan Hunt: Recent Drawings
5–29 April, 1989
BlumHelman Gallery
20 West 57th Street
New York, NY 10019
Copyright © 1989 BlumHelman Gallery
ISBN 0-924008-01-6

Cover
Precipice Drawing I, 1988
graphite and linseed oil on Arches paper
59½ × 45″

Design: Abby Goldstein
Photography: Charles Harrison, Earl Ripling, Ellen Page Wilson
Typesetting: Trufont Typographers
Printing: Colorcraft Lithographers